LADYBUGOLOGY

LADYBUGOLOGY

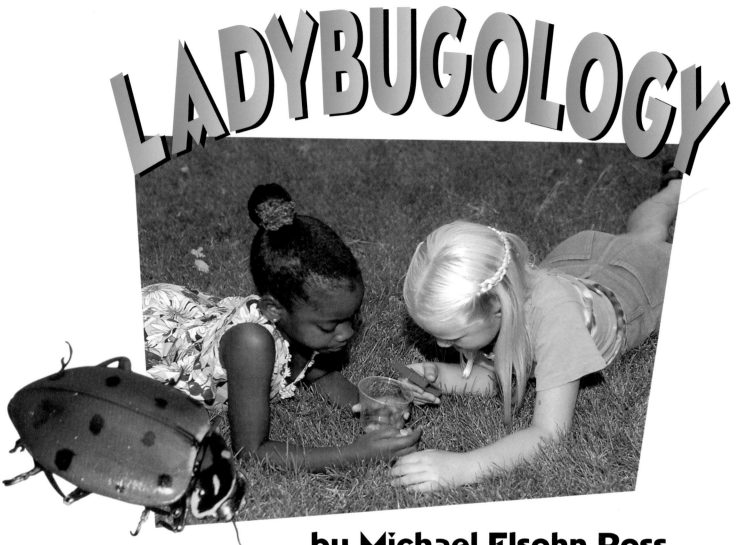

by **Michael Elsohn Ross**

photographs by **Brian Grogan** • illustrations by **Darren Erickson**

3002200069880

Carolrhoda Books, Inc. / Minneapolis

To Davy Douglass and our bug adventures

Special thanks to Carl Brownless, Phyllis Weber, and their students at the El Portal Elementary School, California

Additional photographs courtesy of: © Robert and Linda Mitchell, pp. 27, 28, 30.

Text copyright © 1997 by Michael Elsohn Ross
Photographs copyright © 1997 by Brian Grogan
Illustrations copyright © 1997 by Carolrhoda Books, Inc.

This book is available in two editions:
Library binding by Carolrhoda Books, Inc., a division of Lerner Publishing Group
Soft cover by First Avenue Editions, an imprint of Lerner Publishing Group
241 First Avenue North, Minneapolis, MN 55401 U.S.A.

Website address: www.lernerbooks.com

Library of Congress Cataloging-in-Publications Data

Ross, Michael Elsohn
    Ladybugology / by Michael Elsohn Ross ; photographs by Brian Grogan ; illustrations by Darren Erickson.
        p.   cm.
    Includes index.
    Summary: Describes the physical characteristics, habits, and life of ladybugs and provides instructions for finding, collecting, and keeping these beetles as pets.
    ISBN 1-57505-051-X (lib. bdg. : alk. paper)
    ISBN 1-57505-435-3 (pbk. : alk. paper)
    1. Ladybugs—Juvenile literature. 2. Ladybugs—Experiments—Juvenile literature.
3. Ladybugs as pets—Juvenile literature. [1. Ladybugs. 2. Ladybugs as pets.] I. Grogan, Brian, ill. II. Erickson, Darren, ill. III. Title.
QL596.C65R67 1997
595.76'9—cd21   96-37441

Manufactured in the United States of America
3 4 5 6 7 8 – JR – 06 05 04 03 02 01

Contents

Run a leafy track.

Eat a sugary snack,

like a busy backyard ladybug

with dots all over its back.

You've probably met a ladybug before. Perhaps you know that ladybugs are often red with black dots and they like to crawl around on plants, but what else do you know? Have you ever really been introduced to a ladybug?

Called ladybugs by most folks, these creatures are also known as ladybird beetles. Though they are neither ladies nor birds, they are beetles. Some people are frightened by all little critters like ladybugs, but you'll find that ladybugs don't sting or scratch. They may occasionally give you a nip, but it's nothing that requires a Band-Aid.

Biologists are scientists who study living things. Ornithologists are adventurers who study birds. Ladybugologists are backyard explorers who look into the lives of their ladybug neighbors. They are also scientists who handle small critters with gentleness and respect. You don't need to hurt anything to be a ladybugologist. In fact, the more careful you are with the little creatures, the more you will learn. All you need to do is open your eyes and watch the small bug dramas playing in your own backyard.

Welcome to Ladybug Land

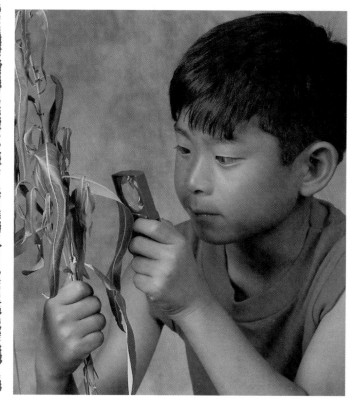

Most folks notice ladybugs because they are as bright and shiny as a fire engine. Ladybugs are easy to see—unless they are resting on a bright red tomato. But a ladybug on a green leaf is hard to miss. During fall and winter in some parts of the world, ladybugs can be found in large clumps in bark crevices, on boulders, or even in old houses or barns. In spring and summer, ladybugs can be seen flying through the air or crawling up and down plants.

To catch your local ladybugs, all you need is a plastic jar (with a lid) and sharp eyes. As you scan leaves, stems, and rocks, focus on any bits of red or orange that you see. Once you spot a

Leaf Patrol

ladybug, swiftly place the open jar beneath the leaf or stem and tap the ladybug into it. Quickly snap on the lid to prevent the ladybug from escaping. As you search for ladybugs, you may also notice small creatures that look like miniature alligators dressed for Halloween. These are young ladybugs, or ladybug **larvae** (LAHR-vee).

Though ladybugs are not hazardous to humans, think about how the people at your house might react to having ladybugs as temporary pets. If your family members are sometimes frightened by small crawling creatures, you may want to show them this article from the famous fictional newspaper *The Busy Bee.*

The Right Visitors

Matilda and Alfie Archer finally found a pet their folks agreed to keep in their modest mobile home in Zolfo Springs, Florida.

"Gators are too big, sharks are too wet, and I can't stand the smell of skunks," declared their dad. "Dogs bark too much, cats scratch too much, and camels spit," explained their mom. "Ladybugs don't eat much. They don't bark, scratch, or spit, and they only stink a teeny-weeny bit," explained Matilda and Alfie as they showed their folks the ladybugs they had discovered in their backyard. Though they were a bit put off by pesky mosquitoes and other bloodsucking bugs, Mr. and Mrs. Archer sighed with relief on seeing the little ladybugs. They were so quiet and cheerful looking that Mr. and Mrs. Archer just couldn't say no—and they didn't!

Ladybugs don't require a motel room, but they do need a place where they will be safe. Are you ready to have some ladybugs as guests? Just follow these simple instructions to create a luxurious ladybug lodge.

Ladybug Lodge

keep it in your room, back porch, or garage. But ladybugs, like most critters, can be harmed by too much heat. A jar left in direct sunlight gets pretty toasty. Cool temperatures can relax your guests, and cool ladybugs can go several days without food (for information on what ladybugs eat, see pages 28 and 30). And no matter how nice your ladybug lodge is, it will never be the same as a ladybug's real home. After your ladybugs have been visiting for a few days, be a good pal and return them to their backyard stomping grounds.

You will need:

- ✔ a clear plastic jar or food container
- ✔ fresh leaves
- ✔ plastic wrap or a plastic bag
- ✔ a rubber band
- ✔ a straight pin
- ✔ a piece of paper or cardboard

1. Place some leaves inside the container.
2. Invite some ladybugs for a visit.
3. Cover the opening with a piece of plastic wrap and secure it with a rubber band. Using a pin, poke some small airholes in the plastic.
4. With the paper or cardboard, make a sign announcing, "Ladybug Lodge," so nobody mistakes it for a plain old container of leaves.

This ladybug lodge will work fine, whether you

Nosy Giant

What if you were the pet of some ten-story-high giant? If your roof was clear, the giant could watch you eat, sleep, and play. For privacy, you could crawl under your bed or make a tent with blankets. Now imagine that you are the giant. This should be simple, since you really are a giant compared to a bug the size of one of your fingernails.

Peek through the roof of the ladybug lodge. What do you see? Keep a piece of paper next to the lodge and jot down every new thing you notice. Though the ladybugs may not be brushing their teeth or watching television, they are probably up to some unusual antics. Are they always doing the same thing, or is there some variety in their routine? Show your list of ladybug activities to some friends, and challenge them to catch sight of the ladybugs doing some different things. Who knows what you may all discover!

You have probably noticed by now that ladybugs are talented climbers. Perhaps they have become tired of the cramped quarters of your ladybug lodge and could use some real exercise in a professional climbing gym. You can construct a climbing gym for your friends in a large plastic dish tub.

Climbing Gym

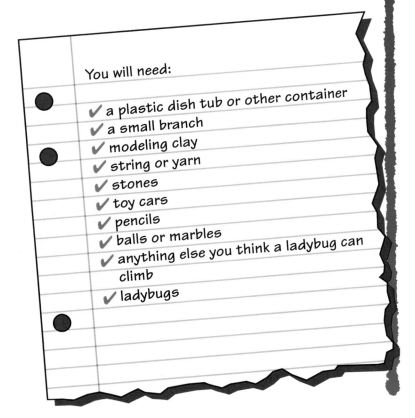

You will need:

✔ a plastic dish tub or other container
✔ a small branch
✔ modeling clay
✔ string or yarn
✔ stones
✔ toy cars
✔ pencils
✔ balls or marbles
✔ anything else you think a ladybug can climb
✔ ladybugs

In your container, arrange some of the items listed to make a world-class climbing gym. Use modeling clay to make a stand for the branch, for some pencils, and for anything else you'd like to make stand up. Tie some string or yarn to your branch for rope ladders. Add any other climbing items to complete your gym. Place the climbing gym outside or in a place where it will be okay if your ladybugs decide to fly.

When your climbing gym is ready, add a ladybug. What does it climb? Can it climb everything? Add a few more ladybugs to the gym. What happens?

Now it's your turn to be a giant jungle gym. Place a ladybug on your arm and watch it. Can it climb over arm hairs? Does it tickle? Be sure to return the ladybugs to their lodge once exercise time is up. Your folks will probably rather have them in the safety of their ladybug home than flying down the hallways.

Are you aware? Would you notice if your best friend wore a wig or if your principal got a tattoo? Would you notice if your father shaved his legs? Do you pick up on small details? Whatever your answers, the Aware Dare is for you. If you are completely tuned out, this game will help you tune in to tiny details. Being tuned in is extremely helpful when you are becoming familiar with new friends, such as ladybugs. If you are sharp-eyed, this game will allow you to show off your keen talents. Though it can be played alone, the Aware Dare is more challenging with two or more players.

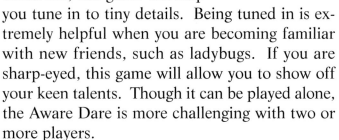

You will need:

✔ one ladybug
✔ a clear drinking glass or plastic container
✔ a magnifying lens
✔ optional: a pen or pencil and paper

How to Play:

1. Place the ladybug on a hard surface, and put the glass or container upside down over it.

2. Decide who is going to go first.

3. Beginning with player number one, take turns sharing ladybug observations. For example, someone might say, "It's red," or "It crawls." Any detail is okay, but no repeats are allowed. More items can be added to someone else's observation, however. For example, someone may have said, "It has dots," but another person can still say, "It has six dots."

Optional: Pick one player to write down what each of you notices.

4. Continue taking turns in the same order until only one player is able to make a new observation. The last person to share a ladybug characteristic is the most aware.

5. Return the ladybug to its lodge.

Before computer math games even existed, there were ladybugs to depend on for mathematical entertainment. No doubt you have counted the dots on a ladybug's back. That's math. Or maybe you have watched a ladybug racing up a plant stem and tried to guess its speed. That's math. Ladybugs are math bugs, and you can get to know them better by trying some of these investigations.

Math Bugs

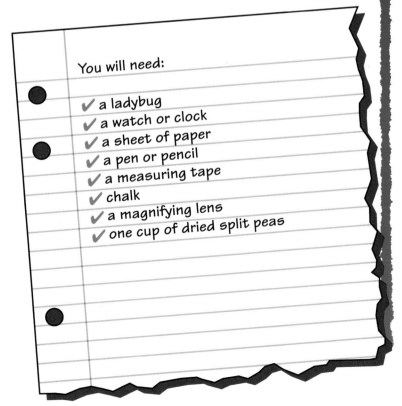

You will need:

✔ a ladybug
✔ a watch or clock
✔ a sheet of paper
✔ a pen or pencil
✔ a measuring tape
✔ chalk
✔ a magnifying lens
✔ one cup of dried split peas

Speed: How fast does a ladybug move? Place one in the middle of a sheet of paper and see how long it takes to crawl off. To see how far a ladybug can go in a minute, let one loose on a large, flat surface, such as a sidewalk. Mark the starting point, then watch the ladybug for one minute. Mark the ending point, then measure the distance between the points. If your ladybug flies away, see if you can measure the distance it travels. How fast can you cover the same distance at a run, walk, or crawl?

Ladybug Lines: Do you always walk in a straight line? Does a ladybug? Place a ladybug on a paved surface and mark its trail with chalk. Try this with several ladybugs and use different colored chalk for each. Look at the chalk lines from above. What do you notice?

Paired Parts: Like people, ladybugs have parts that come in pairs. Make a list of ladybug parts. How many did you come up with? Are there any parts that aren't in pairs? How many?

Patterns: Ladybugs come in special patterns, just like dinner plates. Compare your ladybugs. How many different patterns can you find?

Size: A ladybug is about the same size as a dried split pea. For fun, use split peas to figure out how many ladybugs would fit in a teaspoon, a cup, or in your hand.

Imagine yourself dressed for Halloween as none other than a giant ladybug. To get a preview of what you might look like, draw a picture of yourself in this special costume.

Trick-or-Treat Beetle

Questions, Anyone?: If you wonder about any weird parts you see as you draw your ladybug, jot down some questions, such as, What's that thing hanging down by its mouth, or What's that crack down its back? Your ladybug wonderings may lead to future discoveries.

Bigger than Life: You would be bigger—much bigger—than a real ladybug in your costume. Make your final drawing large. Fill most of the paper. For fun, add some other trick-or-treaters.

Art Show: Dazzle your family and friends with your new creation. Display your picture at the local art museum or neighborhood library, or on the family fridge. Maybe you'll even be a ladybug next Halloween!

You will need:

✔ paper
✔ a pencil
✔ an eraser
✔ watercolors, colored pencils, or crayons
✔ a ladybug

Look closely at your ladybug as you try each of the following activities.

Design Ideas: Like a real costume designer, make some quick, sloppy sketches of your ladybug to figure out the basic shape of the costume and all the parts that will be included.

Color Survey: What colors will you need for your costume? If you're using watercolors, you might try mixing paints to see if you can match the colors of your ladybug.

Do you have any ladybug questions? Here are some questions that kids in my town asked:

Why are ladybugs red? Why do they have spots? Do male and female ladybugs have the same number of spots? Are all ladybugs orange or red?

Do ladybugs have ears? Do they have feelers? How many eyes do they have? How many hearts?

What do ladybugs eat? How do they eat? What eats ladybugs? How fast can ladybugs walk? How fast can they fly? Can they swim? Can they jump? Do they like to walk up or down? How high can they fly? How far do they migrate?

Are there male ladybugs? How do ladybugs attract mates? When do they reproduce? Where do they lay their eggs? How many eggs do they lay? How do ladybugs react to heat? What do they do when they get cold? How strong are their shells? Do they mind bright light? How long do they live? How many different kinds of ladybugs are there?

Wondertime

Are you ready to explore unknown territory? Are you prepared to poke into mysteries? If you are, all you need to do is hold on to a ladybug question. Is there something you really wonder about ladybugs? Yes? Well, let that question lead you on a journey. Below are some tips for questioning ladybugologists.

Follow That Question

—Scrutinize: Could you answer your question through closer observation? For example, if your question was, "Do they have feet?" do you think you might be able to find feet by looking at a ladybug through a magnifying lens?

—Find an Expert: Do you know a bug expert? Perhaps a local gardener, agricultural advisor, or college instructor can give you a hand. Advice may be only a phone call away.

—Research: Other ladybugologists may have already explored your question. Perhaps the answer to your question lies in a book. It may even be in this one. If you don't find the answer somewhere in this book, look at some other books. If that doesn't work, you may need to experiment—read on.

—Experiment: Questions often lead to experiments. Could you answer your questions with an experiment? The chapter starting on page 36 called Kid Experiments has stories about experiments conducted by other bold ladybugologists. They may inspire you to be creative and set up your very own experiment.

Look at this ladybug. Can you find eyes, a nose, or a mouth? Can you find legs, wings, or feet? Do ladybugs have any body parts that are different from yours?

Ladybug Bodies

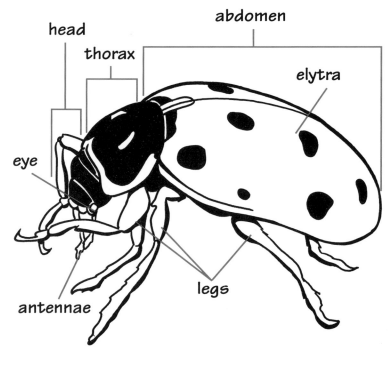

head

thorax

abdomen

elytra

eye

antennae

legs

Peek inside this ladybug. Can you discover a stomach, lungs, or a heart?

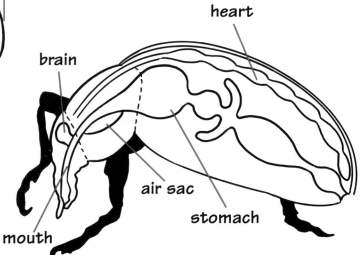

heart

brain

air sac

stomach

mouth

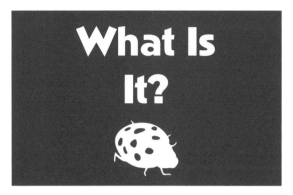

What Is It?

What is spotted like a leopard but lays eggs like a blue jay? What eats like a lion but sleeps in the winter like a bear? What protects itself like a poisonous frog but flies like a firefly? Would you believe—a ladybug? Ladybugs have similarities to all these animals, but their closest relatives are bees, beetles, and flies.

If you have examined ladybugs closely, you may have noticed that they have six legs. Ladybugs are insects, and all insects have six legs. Like other insects' bodies, the ladybug's body is divided into three sections: the head, **thorax,** and **abdomen.**

A ladybug's head is round and hard. The thorax in the middle is where an adult ladybug's three pairs of legs and two pairs of wings are attached. Ladybugs have an inner pair of wings, used for flying, and an outer pair. The **elytra** (EH-luh-truh), or outer pair of wings, are hard like a shell. These outer wings act like a sheath, or covering, to protect the ladybug. Ladybugs are part of the group of animals called **Coleoptera** (koh-lee-OP-teh-rah), which means "sheath wing." A ladybug's abdomen, or end section, is covered by the wings, but you can see it if you turn a ladybug over on its back.

All insects belong to a larger group of animals called **arthropods.** *Arthro* means "joint" and *pod* means "foot." All arthropods have jointed feet. Centipedes, shrimp, daddy longlegs, and sow bugs are all arthropods and distant cousins of the ladybug.

Check out your ladybug and your ladybug drawings. Does your ladybug fit the description of a Coleoptera, an insect, and an arthropod?

Arthropods are creatures with pairs of jointed legs. The animals below are arthropods.

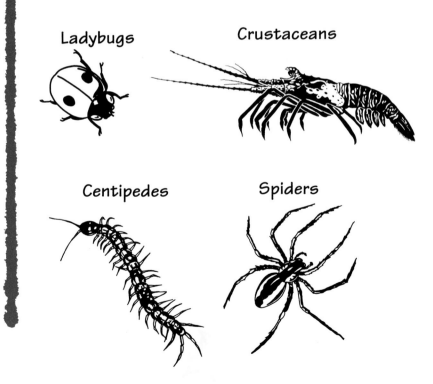

Ladybugs

Crustaceans

Centipedes

Spiders

Insects are arthropods with three body parts and three pairs of legs. The animals below are insects.

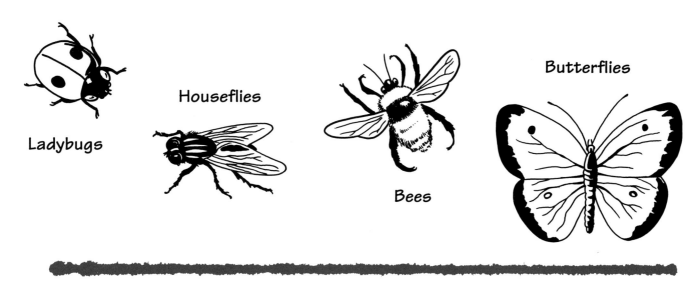

Ladybugs

Houseflies

Bees

Butterflies

Coleoptera are insects with a hard pair of outer wings. The animals below are Coleoptera.

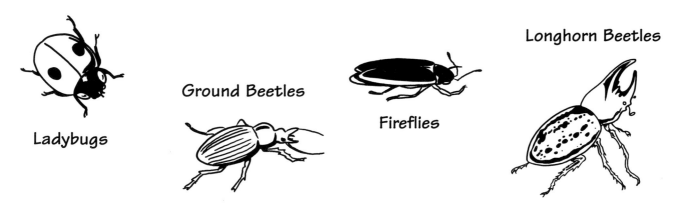

Ladybugs

Ground Beetles

Fireflies

Longhorn Beetles

Each language has its own name for ladybugs. In Polish the word for ladybug is *biedronka*. In Danish the word is *mariehøne.* In Zulu it's *isilkazana esincane.* How do scientists from different countries talk to each other about the little red creature?

Biedronka, Mariehøne... Say What?

To avoid using a variety of names for plants and animals, scientists have devised a worldwide system for naming all living things. Whether you live in Poland, Denmark, or South Africa, each **species,** or kind, of ladybug has just one scientific name.

Latin and Greek, the ancient languages of Rome and Greece, are used in creating scientific names. Most kids already know a few scientific names, because dinosaurs are known by the names given to them by scientists. For example, *Ankylosaurus* is composed of the Greek words *ankylo* (crooked, bent) and *saurus* (lizard). The scientific name for the two-spotted ladybug is *Adalia* (grouping) *bipunctata* (two-spotted), because these ladybugs gather in large groups in the winter and they have two spots.

Other species of ladybugs may have many spots or, like the California ladybug, no spots at all. The yellow-spotted ladybug may have stripes or spots, and some Australian ladybugs are covered with splotchy markings. The polished ladybug is pale yellow with many black spots. Ladybugs also come in different sizes. The smallest are the size of a pinhead, while the largest are as big as a chocolate chip. Since there are more than two thousand species of ladybugs in the world, getting to know them all could take a while.

Aiolocaria hexaspilota

*Rodalia
limbata*

*Rodalia
cardinalis*

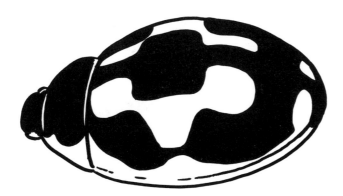

Propylea japonica

Ladybugs have had many names throughout time. In India, they were called Indra's cowherds after the goddess Indra. In England, they have been known as God's little cows or cow ladies, and in France, cows of the Lord. In Sweden, ladybugs are sometimes called Virgin Mary's golden hens. The American name for the bug—ladybug—is also thought to refer to Mary, the mother of Jesus, or "Our Lady." Ladybugs have also been called ladyflies, ladycows, and ladybirds.

In the old days, ladybugs were used to predict the future. In England, people believed they were a sign that crops would be plentiful. Folks in

Ladybug Lore

Central Europe thought that ladybugs meant good weather was on its way. When a ladybug crawled over a young woman's hands, she would say, "The ladybug measures me for my wedding gloves." This ladybug visit was supposed to guarantee a husband within a year.

Not only were ladybugs thought useful for farming and romance, but many people also thought they were a great cure for toothaches. Ladybugs were crushed, then stuffed into cavities. This was rumored to bring instant relief!

Not All Ladies

Even though their name makes it sound as if they are all female, a large number of the ladybugs you find will be male. Some people think that spotted ladybugs are females and unspotted ones are males, but this isn't the case.

It is a common sight to see one ladybug on the back of another. When they are examined from afar, it is hard to tell the difference between the two. But examination through a microscope will show that the ladybug getting a piggyback ride is a male.

Like other male insects, the male ladybug has a special organ, called an **aedeagus** (EE-dee-ah-gus), through which he delivers **sperm** to the eggs of the female. The sperm **fertilize** the eggs, which makes them able to grow. To mate, a male ladybug must climb up on a female ladybug's back. He may remain there for a few hours or even a few days, until mating is completed. A young female ladybug will be ready to mate within a few days of becoming an adult. Most females mate several times during their lifetime.

Once the female's eggs are fertilized by a male, she will lay from two to fifty eggs. Mother ladybugs do not stay around to take care of their young, but they do lay their eggs near the food that the young need to grow big and strong.

Like many other insects, ladybugs go through some major changes as they grow to be adults. Ladybugs begin their lives inside tiny orange or yellow eggs the size of poppy seeds. Female ladybugs deposit these eggs on leaves, on stems, or in bark crevices, and little six-legged orange-and-black larvae hatch from the eggs. These young ladybugs look very different from adult ladybugs. They are long, with narrow tail ends. They don't have the shiny wings of adult ladybugs, and they are splotched rather than dotted. Newly hatched larvae are at their first **instar,** or stage of growth.

After resting for up to a day on their eggshells, the ladybug larvae set out to look for food. They are so hungry, they will eat anything they can get in their jaws, including their brothers and sisters. On a steady diet of little creatures, such as tiny bugs called **aphids** (AY-fehdz), the larvae (seen in photo on right) grow and grow and grow.

Soon the ladybug larvae become so fat, they look as if they will burst. At this time, their skin actually splits and peels off. This process of shedding skin is called **molting.** Once the larvae have molted, they are soft and able to puff out their bodies. Soon after swelling up to a larger size, their new skin hardens. A larva that has molted once is at its second instar. Ladybug larvae usually molt four times, and they have four instars.

Shape Changers

Ladybugs are larvae for one to five weeks, depending on the temperature. The warmer the temperature, the faster the larvae grow. When a larva reaches full size, it is soon ready to change its shape. A larva glues itself to a leaf or other safe location, then sheds its skin for the fourth time.

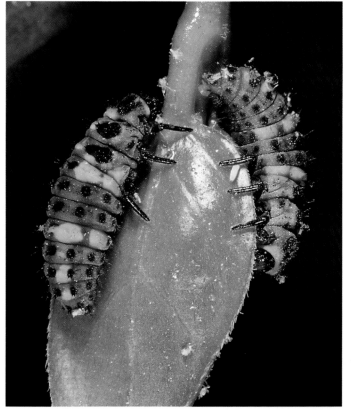

From the skin emerges an orange-and-black **pupa** (PYOO-pah). The pupa is covered by a shell that looks like a legless ladybug. Inside, the pupa is slowly changing into an adult. If touched, the pupa will wiggle, but it cannot go anywhere.

After three to fifteen days, an adult ladybug will climb out of the pupal shell. These adult beetles look so different from the larvae that many people can't believe they are the same creatures. Along with its elytra (hard outer wings), an adult ladybug has a set of underwings used for flight. These underwings are clear. The elytra of freshly emerged adults are light orange and without dots, and the tips of their inner wings stick out from underneath. Within a few hours, dots appear on the elytra and the lower wings are fully tucked under, but the wing color may remain light for months. This makes it easy to tell new adult ladybugs from older ones.

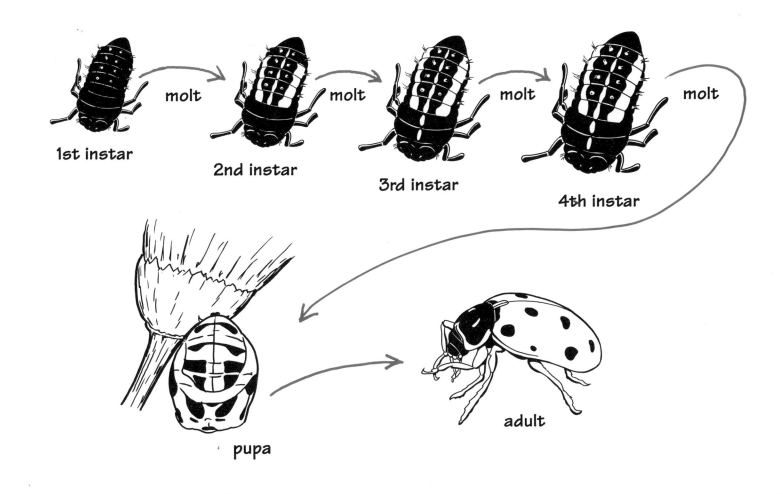

1st instar   molt   2nd instar   molt   3rd instar   molt   4th instar   molt

pupa   adult

You've probably seen herds of cows grazing in meadows, but have you ever seen herds of sap-drinking aphids grazing on leaves? These tiny insects look like water bags with legs and **antennae.** Using needle-like beaks, aphids tap into the sap surging through the stems and leaves of plants. The sap pours in so fast that aphids would blow up like balloons if they didn't release partly digested sap from their back ends. This sweet, sticky sap left behind by aphids is called honeydew. Honeydew is sticky because, like soda pop, it's full of sugar.

Terrors of Leaf Land

Cows provide milk, but their meat may be used for hamburgers. Aphids are also eaten for their meat—it's bugburgers that ladybugs are in search of. An aphid is a perfect snack for a ladybug. Not only is it easy to catch, but it's filled with sweet sap. With its large jaws, a ladybug will munch aphid after aphid until it is full. (You can see a ladybug larva eating aphids in the photo below.) Adult ladybugs may eat as many as one hundred aphids per day. That's a lot of bugburgers!

Ladybugs also dine on tiny armored insects called scales that cover leaves and branches like billions of freckles. Ladybugs eat a variety of bugs, including mites, thrips, mealybugs, very young caterpillars, beetle larvae, and fly maggots. To all of these peaceful leaf munchers, ladybugs are the terrors of leaf land.

Though most ladybugs are meat eaters, some eat plants. The Mexican bean beetle, which is yellow with sixteen black spots, can do serious damage to beans and clover. The squash beetle has fourteen black spots and eats pumpkins and other squashes.

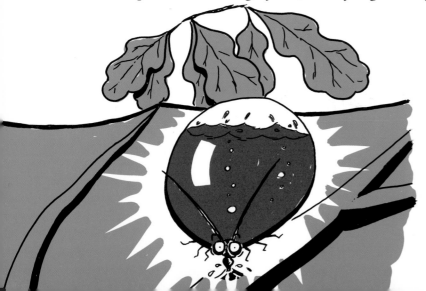

A Plant's Best Friend

In the spring, aphid honeydew can fall from the sky like rain. Living in trees, roses, and other plants are billions and billions of aphids. Aphids can reproduce, or have babies, very quickly. When female aphids are only six days old, they can give birth to baby aphids. With all these aphids being born, it's no wonder that plants can quickly be overrun by sap-drinking aphids.

When people try to kill off aphids with poisons called **pesticides,** it may be only a few days before more aphids fly in from somewhere else. Meanwhile, the pesticides have also killed off ladybugs and other creatures that eat aphids. These predators, or hunters, can't expand their numbers as fast as aphids, so in the end, pesticides really help the aphids.

Long before pesticides were available, farmers depended on ladybugs for bug control. In the 1860s, California was home to many new orchards where oranges, lemons, and other citrus fruits were grown. The climate was perfect, and the farmers were successful—until a small plant-eating insect was accidentally brought in from Australia. This creature was called the cottony-cushion scale because of a white egg sac found on its back. Since it had no predators in California, the cottony-cushion scale spread quickly and killed large numbers of trees. Many farmers just gave up and left their citrus groves.

Fortunately, a clever ladybugologist named Albert Koebele came to the rescue. He searched in Australia for an insect that would eat the scale, and in 1892, he brought back a species of ladybug that dined on cottony-cushion scales and nothing else. Within a year, these ladybugs were heroes. They had saved the orange, grapefruit, and lemon groves. Since that time, ladybugologists have been carefully studying ladybugs to figure out better ways to control insects and other arthropods that eat crops.

A red ladybug on a green leaf stands out like a spotted stop sign. Like a stop sign, the ladybug's red color may also be a warning marker. Hold a ladybug up to your nostrils and take a good whiff. Can you smell anything? Ladybugs give off a bitter odor. When ladybugs are found in large numbers, you can even smell them from a few feet away!

Spotted Stop Signs

Experiments have shown that ladybugs probably aren't too tasty. Some birds, mammals, lizards, toads, and turtles will refuse to snack on ladybugs. Animals that try a ladybug once will usually stay away from them in the future. The bitter smell and bright red color of ladybugs may help remind animals not to have ladybugs for lunch.

Though ladybugs taste terrible to many critters, they are attacked by **parasites,** creatures that feed on living animals. Female parasitic wasps and flies drill holes into ladybug larvae, pupae, or adults, then lay eggs inside. When the eggs hatch, the worm-like wasp larvae begin to munch the ladybug's guts. By the time the wasp larvae change into

pupae, the ladybug is dead. The adult wasps or flies that come out of the cocoon then fly off in search of sweet nectar. Once adult parasites have eaten this high-powered fuel, they have the energy to search for mates and to lay more eggs—in ladybugs.

Ants also attack and sometimes kill ladybugs. Many species of ants feed on honeydew, and to these ants, a ladybug is like a wolf attacking their milk cows. When attacked by ants, most ladybugs will flee. But some species of ladybugs defend themselves by oozing a sticky substance that gums up the ants.

Ladybugs may also be killed off by diseases. In some years, as many as seven out of every ten ladybugs die before winter because of disease or parasites. The ladybugs that survive may reach one year of age, though some Asian ladybugs have lived to the ripe old age of three.

Ladybug, ladybug, fly away home,

Your house is on fire, your children will burn.

In the old days when farmers used fire to clear land for new crops, they would call out this warning to ladybugs. They knew the ladybugs were a help to them in controlling plant-eating insects and didn't want them to be toasted in the flames. Though ladybugs don't have homes like we do, many are found in the same **dormancy** (resting) sites from year to year.

Slumber Party Beetles

In spring and early summer of each year, ladybugs can usually find plenty of aphids and other small bugs to eat. But toward the end of summer, the bug cupboard may become a little bit bare. At this time, many species of ladybugs will fly to cooler locations, such as dark, moist forests or high mountains. The low temperatures in these places cause the ladybugs to slow down. Sloweddown ladybugs don't need to eat much, which helps them survive the winter, when little food is available.

Ken Hagen, a California ladybugologist, studied one species, the convergent ladybug, for many years. He found that convergent ladybugs living along the California coast store large amounts of fat in their bodies, like bears getting ready for winter. The ladybugs use this fat for food during a long winter rest.

Hagen also noticed that when most of the aphids have been eaten up in the fall, convergent ladybugs get ready to leave for better hunting grounds. In the mornings, when the air is still calm, the ladybugs fly straight up, riding the rising air currents. Soon they are so high that it is too cold for them to fly, so they drop into warmer air and fly once more. As they cruise along, they drift with the air currents.

Each day, the ladybugs are carried a little farther, until they reach the Sierra Nevada Mountains. Eventually, they find sunlit spots where they gather in large winter slumber parties. Hagen and other ladybugologists have found piles with as many as 40,000,000 ladybugs!

Ladybug slumber parties are truly cool. Cold winter temperatures chill ladybugs to the point that they can't move or eat. Unlike at a kid's slumber party, there isn't much action. The ladybugs just rest quietly through the winter, living off stored fat, until they are aroused by warmer temperatures. Then the convergent ladybugs ride the winds once more, but this time they travel back down the mountains to the valleys in the west.

Many other species of ladybugs throughout the world besides the convergent ladybug take off on long journeys to resting sites. The ten-spotted ladybug settles down for the winter in hills or mountains on large rocks, heaps of stones, posts, or shrubs. The seven-spotted ladybug prefers cozy resting spots under stones or leaves, or in holes in the ground. Two-spotted ladybugs are often found in bark crevices or cracks in buildings. In late fall, winter, or early spring, you can check out some of these locations. Perhaps you'll find some sleepy ladybugs. If you do, be a considerate neighbor and let them slumber until the warm days of spring.

The students at El Portal Elementary School, my local school in California, explored some of their ladybug questions by devising some fascinating and fun experiments.

Kid Experiments

Will Ladybug Larvae Go to Aphids?

Matteo, Rachel, and David watched two ladybug larvae that they had set in a container with some aphids. One larva walked onto the branch where the aphids were feeding. It passed near an aphid, then walked away. When the ladybug stopped for a while, Rachel thought it was napping. Matteo watched as the larger larva crawled onto the branch. It was heading right toward an aphid. Matteo thought it was going to eat the aphid, but the larva continued to wander around on the leaves. After a few minutes, the larva walked toward an aphid, then swung one of its legs back and forth. Next, the ladybug larva grabbed the aphid with its jaws and began to eat it. Within a couple of minutes, the aphid was completely munched up. Matteo was amazed.

David, Rachel, and Matteo decided that ladybug larvae will go to an aphid, but only when they get close enough to see it. What do you think an adult ladybug would do? Find one and place it with some aphids to see what happens!

What Plants Do Ladybugs Like?

Michelle, Candice, and Stephanie placed ladybugs on the sidewalk and arranged piles of flowers, leaves, and grass in a circle around them. After a while, some of the ladybugs crawled onto the flowers and some went to the grass. Michelle thought that since the ladybugs were crawling on the flowers and grass, they liked them. Do you agree? Why do you think ladybugs would go to grass or flowers?

In another test, Jamie and Josh wanted to see if ladybugs would eat leaves. They placed two ladybugs in a container with a pile of leaves. For fifteen minutes, they watched the ladybugs but didn't see them eat the leaves. They concluded that ladybugs don't like to eat leaves.

Will a Ladybug Fly Off a Pencil?

Allison wondered if ladybugs would fly when they reached the top of a pencil. After watching eleven different ladybugs climb her pencil, this is what she discovered:

Climbed down: 8
Flew Away: 3

Allison thought that the ladybugs may have climbed down because they couldn't see any place to fly to. Do you agree? When she repeated the test using a grass stem, she got mixed results. One ladybug stayed on top, one flew, one fell off, and one walked back down.

How Fast Can a Ladybug Climb?

Ali and Alex stood a yardstick on end, then placed a ladybug at the bottom. It marched right on up as Alex timed it with his watch. The ladybug reached the top in 31 seconds. Rhyen tried the same test, and his ladybug reached the summit in 53 seconds. At the faster rate, a ladybug could climb to the top of a one-hundred-story skyscraper in about three hours! How fast does your ladybug climb?

How Will Ladybugs Escape a Jar?

The thirty-seven ladybugs that Nathan collected in a jar crawled busily and acted like they wanted to get out. Nathan wondered what they would do when he let them go. Would they fly or simply walk away? When Nathan went outside to release them, Denise and Emily joined him to help tally the ladybugs' actions. It was not easy to keep track of the milling ladybugs, but Emily, Denise, and Nathan watched carefully and put tally marks on their data sheet. This is what they found out:

Flew Away: 19
Walked Away: 18

Why do you think some decided to fly and others chose to walk? Do you think you would get the same results?

Which Way Will Ladybugs Climb?

Rebecca wondered if ladybugs would climb horizontally or vertically. She taped two pencils together to make a cross. One at a time, she placed ladybugs on the bottom of the cross. Then she watched to see if they would walk straight to the top or turn off on one of the arms. Rebecca used nine different ladybugs and placed them on the cross five times each. Some ladybugs went mostly to the top, but some went on the arms more often.

Rebecca averaged her results and discovered that ladybugs will choose to go up to the top three out of five times. How do you think this behavior might help ladybugs as they hunt for food or mates?

Can Ladybugs Swim?

To test the swimming abilities of ladybugs, Chris and Josh placed three ladybugs in a container of water. To their surprise, they discovered that all three ladybugs could not only stay afloat, but they even paddled about. Ben, Matt, and Zack placed ladybugs in a pie tin filled with water and noticed that the ladybugs would paddle straight to the edge and climb out. However, when they placed the ladybugs in a jar full of water, the ladybugs were unable to swim to the edge. Though they kept paddling, they couldn't reach the wall of glass. Ben wondered why. What do you think?

In another set of swimming tests, Jeremy found that ladybugs can climb out of the water onto floating objects, such as twigs and leaves. He also discovered that they can swim even when they are upside down!

The Dinner Highway

Most of us don't have sharp-fanged jaguars prowling through our backyards, but we may have some spotted hunters searching for a tasty meal. A British ladybugologist, A. F. G. Dixon, has been studying the hunting behaviors of ladybugs for over thirty years. In the 1950s, Dixon did a series of experiments to discover how ladybugs find the aphids and other small bugs they hunt.

Which way will a ladybug larva go if you place it in the middle of an upright plant stem? Dixon placed larva after larva on stems and found that they almost always went up. He assumed that this behavior helped them reach the tops of branches, where the fresh new leaves (which aphids like) grow.

Dixon also watched ladybug larvae as they searched the undersides of leaves and kept notes on their exact routes. After many tests, he discovered that ladybugs used the veins and edges of leaves as trails. When Dixon examined feeding aphids, he found that they almost always fed near these veins and edges. To ladybugs, leaf veins and edges are highways to dinner.

Ladybugs are busy searchers. They follow stem after stem, vein after vein, until they encounter an aphid, mite, or other delicious bug. Dixon wondered if the number of prey in an area affected the way ladybugs hunted. To find out, he used an upright wooden stick that had measurements marked on it. On his stick, he placed some ladybug larvae that had been recently fed and others that had not had a meal for a while. As he watched the larvae, he kept track of the number of times they changed direction during their climbs up and down the stick.

After testing many ladybug larvae, Dixon found that well-fed larvae change direction often, like a kid who's "it" in a game of tag. This causes them to stay in a small area. Hungry ladybugs, on the other hand, turn less and search over a larger area, like a kid who's "it" in a game of hide-and-seek. This made sense to Dixon. Since aphids and other sap-sucking bugs often live in groups, a ladybug who has just eaten one of these bugs is likely to find another nearby if it keeps turning. Hungry ladybugs search over a larger area until they run into groups of bugs to munch. Once they have had a meal, they then patrol the immediate neighborhood for the rest of the bugs in the colony.

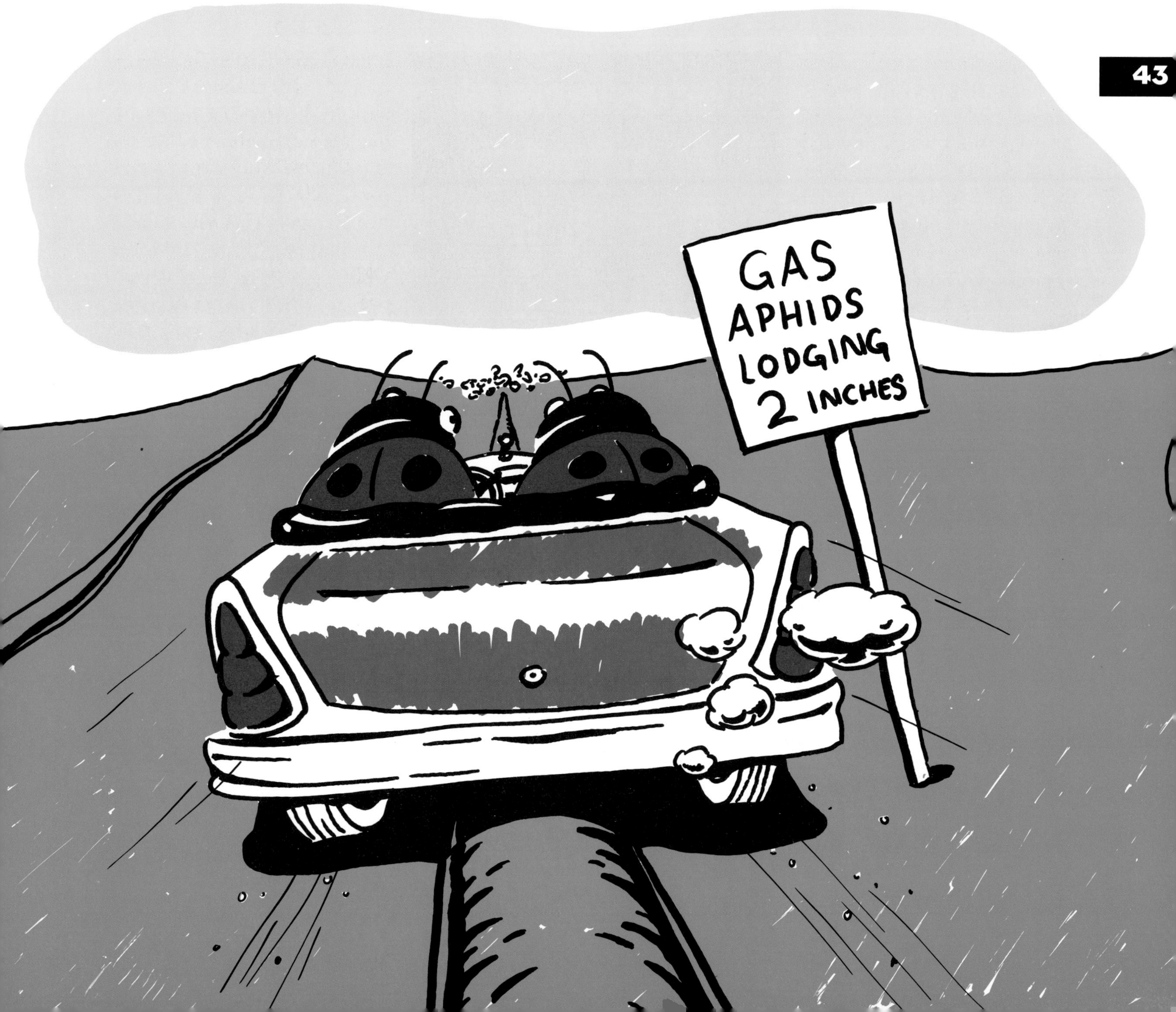
GAS
APHIDS
LODGING
2 INCHES

Although this is the end of the book, it is only the beginning of ladybugology. Remember those questions you jotted down? Are all of them answered? This book could probably not be big enough to answer all the ladybug questions—new questions are asked every day. Did you come up with some new questions as you investigated ladybugs? Maybe no one else has ever asked your questions.

As you have probably discovered, some questions are harder to answer than others. Although they can be frustrating,

Mysteries of a Backyard Buddy

challenging questions sometimes lead to the most exciting adventures. An easily explored question is like a short trip through a familiar place, while a real mystery is like an expedition to a strange and fantastic universe. Consider your unanswered questions once more and imagine the crazy investigations they could lead you into. What are you waiting for? Pack your gear and head out into question land.

Below are some questions that kids in my town may be pursuing at this very instant.

How high can ladybugs fly?

How strong are ladybug's shells?

How do ladybugs attract mates?

Why do they have spots?

Do they mind bright light?

How do they react to heat?

What leftover questions do you have?

Glossary

abdomen: the rear section of an insect's body

aedeagus: the male insect's sexual organ, used to insert sperm into females

antennae: sense organs found on the heads of certain animals, such as insects

aphids: small insects that drink plant sap

arthropods: a large group of animals with jointed legs and segmented bodies

Coleoptera: a group of insects with hard outer wings that includes ladybugs, fireflies, and other beetles

dormancy: a period of sleep or rest

elytra: the hard, shieldlike outer wings of a beetle

fertilize: to cause an egg to develop

instar: a stage of growth in a larva's development

larvae: young insects in an early stage of development

molting: the shedding of skin, fur, or feathers

parasites: animals that live on or in another animal and depend upon it for food

pesticides: chemicals used to kill insects and other animals

prey: animals that are hunted and eaten by others

pupa: the stage of an insect's life in which it changes from a larva into an adult

species: a group of animals with common traits, especially the means of creating young

sperm: the fluid that fertilizes a female's eggs

thorax: the middle section of an insect, where legs or wings may be attached

Index

About the Author

For over twenty years, Michael Elsohn Ross has taught visitors to Yosemite National Park about the park's wildlife and geology. Mr. Ross, his wife, Lisa (a nurse who served nine seasons as a ranger-naturalist), and their son, Nick, have led other families on wilderness expeditions from the time Nick learned to crawl. Mr. Ross studied conservation of natural resources at the University of California/Berkeley, with a minor in entomology (the study of insects). His other books for children include the Naturalist's Apprentice series, also published by Carolrhoda.

Mr. Ross makes his home on a bluff above the wild and scenic Merced River, at the entrance to Yosemite. His backyard garden is a haven for rolypolies, crickets, snails, worms, caterpillars, ladybugs, and a myriad of other intriguing critters.